WE'RE TALKING ABOUT
SMOKING

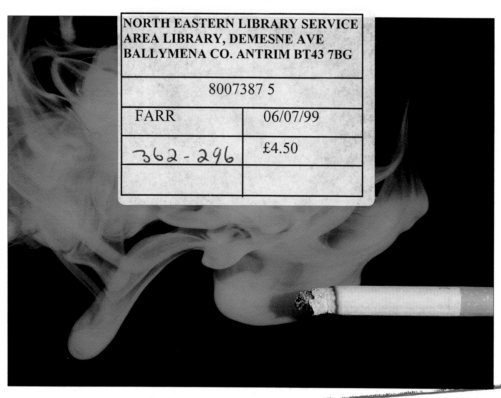

KAREN BRYANT-MOLE

Wayland

Editor: Catherine Baxter
Design: John Christopher
Illustration: John Yates

This edition published in 1997 by Wayland Publishers Ltd

First published in 1995 by Wayland Publishers Ltd
61 Western Road, Hove, East Sussex, BN3 1JD, England

Find Wayland on the internet at http://www.wayland.co.uk

British Library Cataloguing in Publication Data

Bryant-Mole, Karen
We're Talking About Smoking
1. Smoking – Juvenile literature
2. Tobacco habit – Juvenile literature
I. Title II. Yates, John, 1939 – III. Smoking
362.296

Paperback ISBN 0 7502 2118 6

Typeset by Strong Silent Type, England
Printed and bound in Italy by G. Canale & C.S.p.A., Turin

Picture Acknowledgements
Advertising Archives 15; Ace 5 (Anne Purkiss), 10 (bottom, Maritius),
20 (Zephyr Pictures), 24 (Bo Cederwall); Chapel Studios cover, title
page, 4, 6, 10 (top), 13, 18, 19, 21 (bottom), 22, 23, 25, 28 (bottom),
29 (bottom); Sally & Richard Greenhill 8, 11 (top), 26 (top); Science
Photo Library 7 (top, Martin Bond), 16 (Dr E. Walker), 17 (Mark
Clarke), 21 (Blair Seitz); Tony Stone Worldwide 12 (Penny Tweedie),
14, 26 (bottom, Peter Correz), 28/29 (Chuck Keeler), WPL 27.

Most of the people who are featured in this book are models.

Contents

Choices

Josie and her friends were sitting around trying to imagine what life would be like when they were grown up. They all thought that one of the best things would be that they could choose what they wanted to do instead of having to do what they were told.

But then Emma said that not everyone made the right choices. Her big sister had just started smoking. She had chosen to start smoking but Emma thought that it was a bad choice.

Matt agreed. He said he had read that, every year, over 100,000 people in Great Britain were killed by smoking. They all thought that sounded like a lot of people but no one was really sure how many 100,000 was. Emma thought it was about the same as the number of children in a big school.

▼ Matt, Josie and Emma talked about growing up.

▲ Each year, smoking kills more people than you can see here.

Matt thought it was about the same as the number of people at a football match. But 100,000 is a much, much larger number than that. In fact, it is about ten times the number of people you can see in the picture above. And that is a lot of people.

Josie and her friends were right to say that part of growing up is about being able to make choices for yourself. But it can sometimes be difficult to make the right choices, especially if you don't have enough information. Emma thought that her sister had made the wrong choice when she decided to start smoking. This book will tell you all about smoking and about the harm that it can do. Hopefully, you will agree with Emma.

What's in cigarette smoke?

There are three main ingredients in cigarette smoke that are bad for our bodies and which can cause illnesses and diseases. These are: nicotine, carbon monoxide and tar.

▼ Even if you don't smoke, the poisonous fumes from other people's cigarettes can damage your lungs.

Nicotine

When a smoker breathes in the cigarette's smoke, the smoke goes into his or her lungs. The nicotine in the smoke goes into the smoker's blood. Nicotine in the blood makes a person's heart pump more strongly and beat faster. The heart is having to work harder than it should.

Tar

Tar is the sticky black stuff that is used to mend roads or that you sometimes see on the beach. You can't see the tar in smoke but if you breathe it in, the tiny droplets of tar lie on the lining of the lungs. This causes terrible damage to lungs. The more a person smokes the more tar there will be in the lungs.

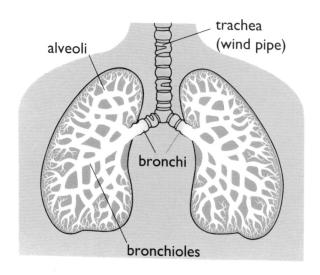

▲ This is what your lungs look like.

Carbon monoxide

Carbon monoxide is the same poisonous gas that comes out of a car's exhaust pipe. Blood usually has lots of oxygen in it. In smokers' blood some of that oxygen is replaced by the poisonous carbon monoxide. This makes the blood less healthy and can lead to the arteries, which are the tubes that carry your blood, becoming blocked.

Carbon monoxide is found in ▶ exhaust fumes and cigarette smoke.

Illnesses and diseases

Smoking doesn't just make you less healthy than a person who doesn't smoke. Smoking can kill.

Smoking makes your heart work too hard, particularly if your arteries become blocked. A smoker is about three times more likely to die from heart diseases, such as a heart attack, than a non-smoker of the same age.

Blocked arteries can cause other problems too. If an artery is blocked the blood won't be able to get through to the part of the body that it is supposed to supply.

Sometimes the blood manages to find other smaller arteries and uses those. If it can't, the part of the body that the blood is trying to get to may start to die off.

More than three-quarters of deaths from lung cancer are caused by smoking. The more cigarettes people smoke the more likely they are to get lung cancer. Most doctors think that it is the tar in cigarettes that causes lung cancer.

▼ Smoking is dangerous. It can kill.

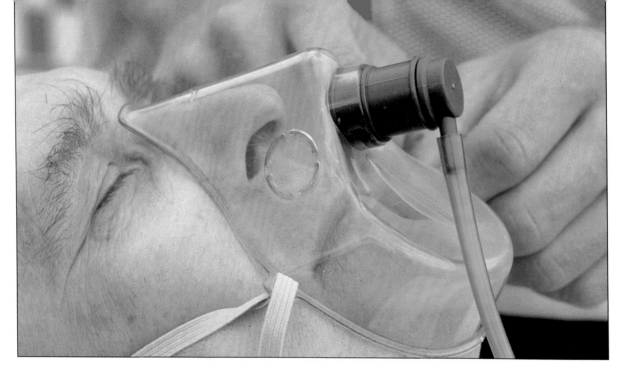

▲ People with lung diseases may need to be given oxygen.

Smoking also causes other lung diseases. About three-quarters of deaths from lung diseases such as bronchitis and emphysema are caused by smoking. Lung diseases like these are caused by smoke damaging the lining of the lungs.

Many of the people who eventually die from diseases caused by smoking are ill for a very long time. A person suffering from heart disease may spend years hardly being able to walk more than a few steps without becoming breathless.

Someone with bronchitis may even find breathing difficult. Lots of people with smoking-related diseases will have to spend days, weeks or even years in hospital.

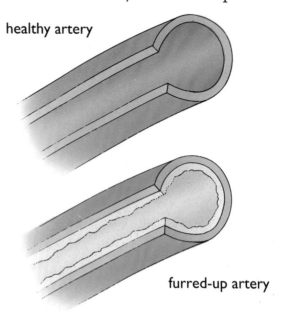

healthy artery

furred-up artery

Smoking can block up arteries. ▶

Young smokers

Diseases like lung cancer and bronchitis usually affect older people who have been smoking a lot of cigarettes for many years. But even young people who have not been smoking for long may find that they are not as healthy as they used to be.

Many young smokers develop a chesty cough. This is sometimes called 'smoker's cough'. People with smoker's cough often cough up a small amount of thick fluid from their lungs, especially when they wake up in the mornings. Their bodies have made this fluid to line their lungs, to try to protect them from the harmful smoke.

Lots of young smokers find that they become breathless when they are doing sport or even just running for a bus. Some stop smoking. Others stop doing sport.

The cost of a packet of cigarettes a ▶ day for six months is more than the cost of a holiday abroad.

Bodies need exercise to keep healthy. A smoker who does no exercise is going to be much less healthy and fit than an active non-smoker. Exercise doesn't have to mean football or netball. Dancing, cycling and even walking are all ways of keeping fit.

◀ Smoking can give people a chesty cough.

▲ Cycling is one way to keep your body healthy.

Smoking isn't just unhealthy. It is also very smelly. Smoking makes your mouth smell, your hands smell, your clothes smell and your hair smell. Do you really want to smell like an old ashtray? Smoking is also expensive.

Selling cigarettes to young people under the age of sixteen is illegal. That means that it is against the law. The main reason for this is that smoking is very harmful, particularly to young, growing bodies.

Friends

As you get older you will probably find that friends play a more important part in your life. Many children like to dress like their friends, talk like their friends and do the same things that their friends are doing. It feels good to belong to a group in this way.

But what if one of the things this group is doing is smoking?

Sometimes people go along with what the group does, not because they want to but because they are scared that their friends won't like them any more, or because they don't want to look silly.

Sam's friends, Thomas and Craig, tried to get Sam to smoke a cigarette. When he said no they started to laugh at him and said he was a wimp. This made Sam feel terrible. But then he thought about why he didn't want the cigarette. He told his friends he thought it was a crazy idea to go around damaging your body on purpose. He asked Thomas and Craig why they thought he should

▼ Friends often like doing the same types of things.

▲ At first, Thomas and Craig laughed at Sam.

smoke the cigarette. Thomas and Craig just looked at each other and shrugged. They couldn't think of one good reason.

If someone laughs at you because you don't want to smoke, try explaining why. Giving reasons is a much easier way of dealing with the situation than just saying you don't want to.

And it might make the person who asked you to smoke look the silly one, not you.

If someone says he or she won't be your friend unless you have a cigarette, ask yourself whether a true friend would say this. A person who tries to make you do something you don't want to is not a real friend.

Selling cigarettes

Any company that makes something wants people to buy what it makes. To get people to do this, it advertises. Adverts on television, in cinemas, on radio, in magazines and on posters try to persuade us to buy what they are making.

In the past, cigarette manufacturers were allowed to advertise on television. Television advertising is very effective. You have probably wanted to buy something that you have seen advertised on television.

People began to get worried about this. It was felt that the adverts didn't just make smokers decide which type, or brand, of cigarette to smoke but actually made non-smokers start smoking.

People were also unhappy that something that caused diseases and even killed could be advertised in this way. And so the advertising of cigarettes on television was stopped.

Cigarette manufacturers still need to find ways of getting as many people as possible to hear of their product. So, now they sponsor events that are on television.

Sponsoring an event means that the company gives some money so that the event can take place. Cricket, motor racing, horse racing and sailing are amongst the many activities that are, or have been, sponsored by cigarette companies. When the event is shown on television everyone can see the cigarette company's posters and, often, the commentator keeps mentioning the name of the company.

▲ Cigarette advertising is banned on British television, but you still see adverts on billboards.

Cigarette companies would say that, without their money, these events would never take place and that they bring enjoyment to lots of people. Some people might say that the companies are just trying to get more people to smoke their cigarettes and that linking unhealthy cigarettes with sport is wrong.

◄ Cigarette manufacturers often sponsor sports events.

Why start?

Some young people start smoking because they think it makes them look grown up.

But doing something that at the very least will make you less fit and at worst could kill you, isn't a very grown-up decision to make. And the fact is that it is grown ups who are stopping smoking. Every week, thousands of grown ups decide that what they are doing is dangerous and a waste of money and they give up. Grown ups know it doesn't make you look grown up.

Some people smoke because they think it makes them look cool. But do you really think that smelling of old smoke is cool? And is it cool to worry about what you look like on the outside but not on the inside? A smoker's lungs certainly don't look cool.

Other people smoke because they say it stops them feeling worried or nervous. But smoking isn't solving the problem. It's hiding it. When you have finished the cigarette you will just start feeling worried or nervous again.

▼ This is a section of a lung that has been damaged by smoking.

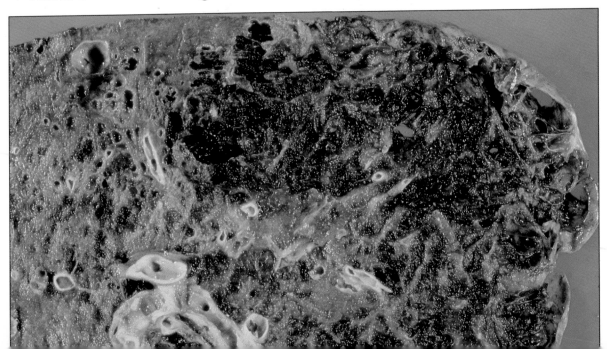

▲ Smoking does not make you thin.

What are you going to do? Have another one?

Everyone gets worried or anxious from time to time but there are better ways to deal with this than by smoking. Talking to someone else about how you are feeling is often a good start.

Some people smoke because they think it will make them thin. Smoking does not make you thin. If it did, everyone who smoked would be thin. But they aren't. Smokers come in all shapes and sizes, in just the same way that non-smokers do.

Passive smoking

You might feel that, because you don't smoke and because you don't think you will ever start smoking, you don't have anything to worry about. But it is not just smokers who breathe in smoke. Most of the smoke from a cigarette goes into the air. This means that other people can breathe in the smoke too whether or not they are smoking themselves. Breathing in the poisonous smoke from other people's cigarettes is called passive smoking.

Passive smoking can affect different people in different ways. Some people find that they get a headache or start coughing if they are in a smoky room. It may cause dizziness, sneezing or red eyes. Other people find that it gives them problems with their breathing. Many people find being in a smoke-filled room uncomfortable. And, when they leave, they find that their hair and clothes smell of the smoke from other people's cigarettes.

Someone who spends a lot of time in very smoky places may even develop the same diseases as a smoker. Although it is quite unusual, people have died from diseases that they probably got through passive smoking.

◀ Many people dislike breathing in other people's smoke.

▼ This sign means 'No Smoking'.

Efforts are now being made to make some places smoke-free. Passengers are not allowed to smoke on most trains and most buses. Many people feel that this is a good thing. They do not see why they should have to breathe in other people's smoke. Some smokers feel that this is not fair. They do not see why they should be told where they can or can't smoke. What do you feel?

Babies and young children

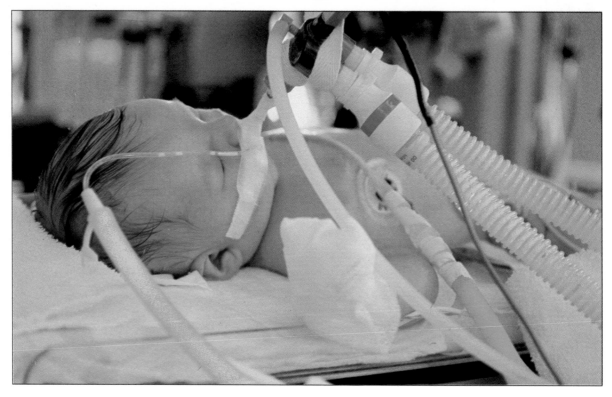

▲ This small baby needs very special care.

Smoking can affect babies even before they are born. Mothers who smoke are more likely to give birth to small babies, who may need special care and attention, than mothers who don't smoke. This is probably because the mother's blood, which passes between the mother and baby while it is growing inside her, is not as healthy as the blood of a non-smoking mother. The baby does not grow as well, or as much, as it should.

The time that the baby is growing inside the mother is called the pregnancy. Mothers who smoke are more likely to have problems with their pregnancy than those who don't. It could even lead to the baby dying before it is born.

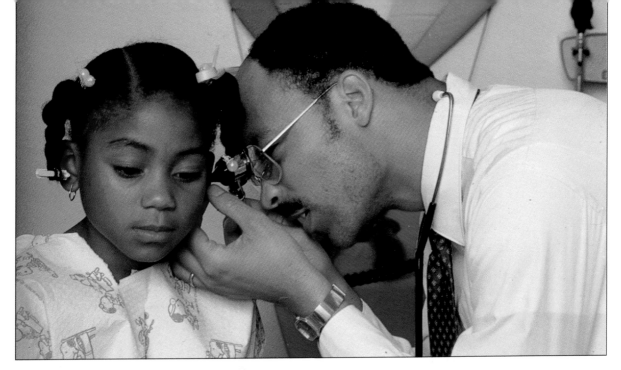

▲ The doctor is examining this girl's ears.

Living in a smoky home causes problems for some children. Babies are more likely to get breathing problems than those living in a smoke-free home. It also seems that children who live with someone who smokes are more likely to have ear, nose and throat problems too.

Children who have breathing problems, such as asthma, are often made worse by living in a house where people smoke.

Very young children like to touch everything they see. Often they put what they pick up into their mouths. Tobacco is poisonous if it is swallowed. A toddler who picked up a cigarette end from an ash tray and ate it would probably be sick. A toddler who found a packet of cigarettes and ate a whole cigarette could die.

Old cigarette ends ▶ can be dangerous.

Addiction

Many people who start by smoking just one or two cigarettes a week find that they soon begin to smoke more and more and end up smoking a number of cigarettes every day.

▲ Being addicted to cigarettes makes some people get cross easily.

Part of the reason that this happens is because nicotine, one of the main ingredients in cigarettes, is a drug. Once a person has started to use nicotine, his or her body gets used to it. And, even though it is harming the body, the body starts to need it. Needing a drug like this and not being able to live without it is called addiction. Many smokers are addicted to cigarettes.

Being addicted to cigarettes has a number of effects. If a smoker does not have a cigarette for a while, he or she may start to feel anxious or in a bad mood or unhappy. Smokers may find that they get cross easily or can't relax. The smoker feels that the only way to get over these feelings is to have another cigarette. And so it goes on.

The worst part about being addicted to cigarettes is that smokers are no longer in charge of their own bodies. The cigarettes have taken over. Even smokers who aren't addicted often find that smoking becomes a habit that is hard to break. They get used to smoking at certain times of the day and in certain places.

So, whenever they are in those situations they light up a cigarette almost without thinking.

The best way to avoid the problem of smoking becoming a habit or even an addiction is never to start smoking at all.

▼ This man always has a cigarette with his cup of coffee.

Stopping smoking

Although smoking quickly becomes a habit and may lead to someone becoming addicted to cigarettes, people can, and do, manage to give up smoking. Stopping smoking is good in many ways. People who stop smoking have more money as they are not wasting it on cigarettes. Almost straight away, they will start to feel healthier too. They won't smell of old smoke any more either. And, best of all, if they stop before getting any of the most serious diseases linked to smoking, their chance of getting those diseases gets less and less the longer they stay away from cigarettes.

Nicotine patches can help people ▶ to give up smoking.

◄ Giving up smoking makes most people feel heathier.

But giving up isn't always easy. Some people think that it doesn't matter if they smoke when they are young because they will always be able to give up when they are a bit older. It isn't as simple as that.

People find it difficult not to smoke at times or in places where they have always smoked. Their bodies have got used to the nicotine. They may feel desperate for a cigarette. Some people give in and start smoking again. Others keep going and eventually find that they can live without cigarettes.

People who find giving up smoking really difficult can get help. There are courses to go on and leaflets to read. And there are products that they can buy that aren't cigarettes but that contain nicotine. These allow smokers to cut down the amount of nicotine in their bodies gradually instead of just stopping it suddenly. Of course, if you don't start, you won't have to go through any of this, will you?

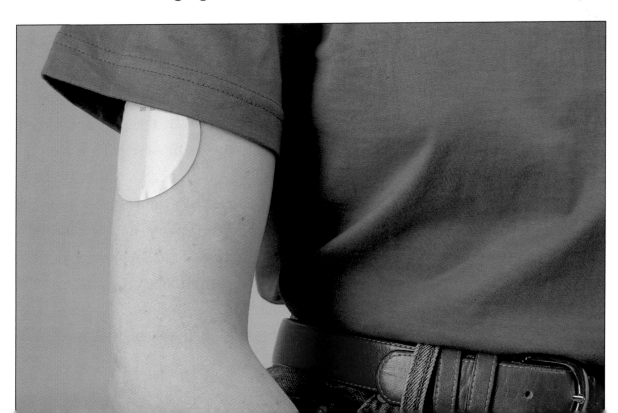

My life

These people know about some of the bad effects of smoking. Two of them have given up and one wishes he could.

'My friends and I all smoked. We thought we looked really grown up. Once we were at a disco and this boy asked me to dance. Then he said that he liked the way I danced but he didn't like the way I smelled! I was so embarrassed. When you smoke you can't really tell that you smell. Other people can though. I gave up after that. I didn't want people to think I was smelly.'

▲ A boy told Louise she smelled horrible.

'A mate gave me my first cigarette. That first puff was horrible. It made me feel sick. My mate said that once I got used to cigarettes this feeling would stop. He was right. But soon I couldn't live without cigarettes. Now I smoke about a packet a day. I hate the way cigarettes have taken over my life. I've tried giving up three times but each time I start again. I can't seem to live without cigarettes. I wish I had never started.'

◄ Mark is addicted to cigarettes.

'A friend suggested going to a keep fit class. I thought it sounded fun. But ten minutes into the class I was puffing and panting and had to sit down. My friend was still leaping around! I had been meaning to stop smoking. I had a terrible cough and I used to get out of breath really easily. At first it was very difficult to give up. But my friend kept telling me how well I was doing. Now I can do the whole class, no problem! You wouldn't believe how much better I feel since giving up.'

▼ Jo feels much fitter now.

The future

Everyone knows that smoking is bad for you, yet some people still take up smoking and many smokers carry on smoking. Now that the risks of passive smoking are becoming more widely known it isn't just smokers who need to worry about cigarettes. Smoking affects everyone.

▲ Smoking is banned in this office.

▲ Stopping can be difficult.

Action is being taken to keep the air that we breathe as clean as possible and to stop us having to breathe in cigarette smoke if we don't want to. As well as being banned on many trains and buses, smoking is also banned in most cinemas and theatres. Many of the offices where people work are now smoke-free too. In the future more places may become smoke-free.

But the most effective way to have fewer people damaging their bodies is to help young people choose never to smoke. Fewer young smokers means, eventually, fewer adult smokers. Fewer adult smokers means fewer people getting ill and dying.

You now know about the harm that smoking can cause. If you are offered a cigarette, stop and think. Am I making the right choice?

▼ What would you say?

People who are already smokers need to be encouraged to stop smoking. Stopping smoking can be hard and smokers sometimes make up excuses about why they can't or don't want to give up. The first few weeks are often the most difficult. If you know someone who is trying to stop smoking, give him or her plenty of praise. Telling people how well they are doing helps them to feel good about themselves and may make the difficult times easier.

Glossary

Addicted When the body can't do without something.

Arteries Tubes that send blood around the body.

Banned Something that is not allowed.

Brand A particular make of something.

Bronchitis Swelling of the air passages in the lungs.

Carbon monoxide A very poisonous, colourless gas.

Commentator Someone, on television or radio, who describes action to the audience.

Company A group of people who run a business together.

Emphysema A disease that damages the linings of the lungs.

Fluid Liquid, the opposite of solid.

Illegal Against the law.

Manufacturer A company or person that makes things.

Nicotine A poisonous substance found in tobacco.

Oxygen A colourless gas that is found in air. It is necessary for healthy blood.

Passive smoking Breathing in other people's cigarette smoke.

Poisonous Something that can harm or even kill you.

Product The type of thing that the manufacturer makes.

Sponsor Give money to pay towards an event.

Tar A thick, dark liquid.

Further information

Books to read

Why do People Smoke? by Pete Saunders (Watts, 1994)
What do you know about Smoking? by Pete Saunders (Watts, 1994)
We're Talking About Drugs by Jenny Bryan (Wayland, 1995)

If you would like to find out more about smoking and the harm that smoking can do, the Health Education Authority (address below) produces a number of useful leaflets, including: *Smoking. The Facts, Passive Smoking, Stopping Smoking* and *Stopping Smoking Made Easier.*

Useful Addresses

Health Education Authority, Hamilton House, Mabledon Place, London WC1H 9TX   Tel: 0171 383 3833

Action on Smoking and Health (ASH), 5–11 Mortimer Street, London W1N 7RH   Tel: 0171 637 9843

Anyone who wants to give up smoking can speak to his or her doctor, who will give advice and will have details of local courses, self-help groups and treatments available.

Index